THE ABUNDANT LIFE

Practical Wisdom for
Spiritual Mastery

Almine

Published by Spiritual Journeys LLC

Copyright 2009 MAB 998 Megatrust

By Almine
Spiritual Journeys LLC
P.O. Box 300
Newport, Oregon 97365

Cover Illustration — Dorian Dyer
Graphic Artist — Eva Pulnicki

www.yogaofillumination.com
(877) 552-5646

Manufactured in the United States of America

ISBN 978–1–934070–20–8 (Softcover)
ISBN 978-1-934070-21-5 (Adobe Reader)

Table of Contents

Endorsements

About the Author

Almine is widely regarded as the leading mystic of our time. Author of 11 books and originator of the globally acclaimed healing modality, Belvaspata, she shares her wisdom with a rapidly growing world-wide audience on a daily basis.[1]

Her profound wisdom and unparalleled inter-dimensional abilities have been acclaimed by scientists and students alike.

---

1 See http://alminediary.com/, http://www.facebook.com/SeersWisdom and http://twitter.com/alminewisdom

Introduction

(Excerpt from Almine's Journal dated January 2010)

"Long have I searched through space and time for the highest wisdom I could find. I thirsted for light to banish the night but a contradiction did I find. Light is one part of two separate poles — the brighter it shines the dimmer frequency grows.

Wisdom I did find, but it nourishes the mind when it is based on perception alone. Unless it is felt with the heart, love and compassion grow cold.

Like a ladder it is that reaches for the sky, but only so far can it go. Then one must fly into that which cannot be known. Beyond, indivisible life awaits. Wisdom leads one but to the unknowable's gates.

My thirst is quenched; my search is done, but the rapturous adventure has just begun — to discover the paradoxical embrace of the One."

Accessing Abundance

To live within the Infinite's
Being is to live in the fullness
of an inexhaustible supply.
Acknowledging the never-
ending Source of abundance
increases its accessibility.

Most who seek abundance focus on their
perceived lack and thereby strengthen it.
See yourself as part of the abundance of
Creation. There are trillions of field flowers,
grains of sand, stars. Your body too consists
of abundant life. Let your affirmation be:
"I am abundance."

We promote abundance by being abundant
with ourselves. If we feel guilty about
having more than others, we deprive
not only ourselves but them as well.

Success and abundance are the only constants
in life. We either align ourselves with them
through surrender and trust, or cut ourselves
off from them through opposing life.

To desire to live abundantly is as natural
as the fish desiring the ocean. Money
is only a small part of abundance.

The true currency of an abundant
life is elegance and grace born of
self-respect. It is available to all.

Abundance is living within your
means with grace. It has nothing to
do with how much you earn.

Acknowledgement of the Source of all
abundance as our self giving to our self
increases the flow.

Our being is our source of limitless supply.
We are heirs to the One Life's supply —
wealthy beyond our wildest dreams.

A positive attitude begets increase. With a surrendered embrace of life, the pushing away of resources will cease. Centripetal force, the result of an inclusive attitude, pulls all towards you for a life of plenitude.

Asking for abundance while ignoring present blessings closes the ability to receive. Welcome each new day the way a flower unfolds in the sun, that the ability to receive may be yours.

Abundance comes to one who lives in fullness.
Fullness comes from inclusive vision, gratefully embracing the validity of every part of life.

The drive for acquisition is the opposite of the
fullness of life abundant, for it presupposes a
lack. It is the little self that feels incomplete.
The large Self knows its own fullness.

Our being is an endless ocean of supply.
Our attitudes are its sluices. Through
inclusive living those sluices open.

Take moments in your day to assess
your abundant resources; the joy of
accomplishment, the love of a child. Then
you will find you are wealthy indeed.

Since acceptance is the first step to change,
seeing yourself as abundant in the moment is
important to increasing abundant resources
for the future. Take time each day to
acknowledge your abundance with gratitude.

When you receive and hoard, you
have become the tomb of abundance.
When you receive and give, you are
the womb of abundant flow.

All blessings to come begin by acknowledging gratefully present gifts.
It decreases our supply when we focus
on lack, instead of what we have.

Seeking abundance is a bottomless pit when
it is defined as increase. We live in elegant
sufficiency when we gratefully recognize we
have all we need.

Living a fully conscious life of wholesome
values puts substance behind our
endeavors. Soulless activity is hollow
and cannot support abundance.

Think of money as love. Give freely where
you can, and it shall return freely.

Knowing the Earth to be our source of supply,
and our being to be our sustenance, we have
established the foundation for prosperity.

Each day life presents doors for you to knock
on. Be alert for these multiple opportunities.
Some may open and some may not, but knock!

Give that you may get. One who
generously assists wherever possible
opens the sluices of cosmic supply.

What we appreciate, we activate within by
resonating with it. What we are grateful
for, we increase through empowering it.
Appreciation and gratitude jointly heighten
our capacity to receive life's bounty.

As you wish for abundance, ask for
the world if that is what you want. If
your desire is not met, no matter — it
was not a need but a preference.

See yourself as the steward of your possessions. Treat them with respect, and repair
rather than replace whenever practical.

Live life as a work of art. Let an
attitude of graceful creativity
enliven your financial affairs.

It is through asking for what we want while
appreciating what we have, that we live
the most powerful law of abundance.

Spend money as a proxy. As you give a dollar
to a person in need, give it by proxy through
intention to all others who are in need.

Frugality has nothing to do with how much
money we spend, but in how impeccably we
refuse to squander the energy it represents.

Neither abundance nor poverty
exists within the Ocean of Life.
When we know this, we are free.

Greed is born of seeing resources as
limited, which in turn comes from
living a life of boundaries.

Contemplate with praise the abundance of
the stars, the snowflakes, the field flowers.
For what you focus on, you become.

We dwell in abundance, limited only by our
inability to recognize what is available.

Dissolving Barriers to Abundance

Barriers of limitation seem as
thick as concrete to us. This is
due to our belief systems. When
we see behind the appearances,
they effortlessly dissolve.

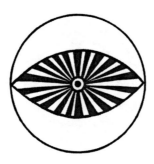

Spend only what you have so that you do not
become the slave of dysfunctional needs.

As the One Life, we are all things. There
is nothing to become. When we strive for
more, we perpetuate impoverishment.

Some acquire to live, others live to acquire. In both instances acquisition has
become a need rather than a joy.

To regret the loss of resources or possessions
is to deny that we are the creators of our life
and can create as much abundance again.

Vigorously uproot belief systems that
indoctrinate through perceived status
symbols and fabricated needs.

When we see monetary resources
as our security, we deny that our
being is our sustenance.

The belief that money has to be
earned reduces the possibility that
it can come from other sources.

Considering the worth of the recipient of our
gifts is to close the conduits of our own supply,
for to deny another's worth is to deny our self.

Resistance to life is a centrifugal force
pushing bounty away as resources
spin outwards within our space.

When we deplete our physical resources, our
abundance dwindles as well. Fatigue comes
from resistance to life. Fatigue indicates that
impeccability of vision is required, not more
rest, for we can rest while we work and
work while we rest.

Do not give strength to the illusion of past
losses. In the flawlessness of life no loss
can occur that is not fully compensated. In
pure beingness where no opposites exist,
neither loss nor compensation is real.

Only in duality do problems exist. A problem
only exists because its solution is already
there, for each is defined by its opposite.
When we live in the One Life, neither
problems nor solutions have any reality.

Money represents crystallized power.
If you spend it with guilt, the presence
of guilt in your life is empowered.

Focusing on lack instead of supply promotes
depletion. All blessings come through
gratefully acknowledging present gifts.

Eliminating mind that judges and divides requires complete surrender to life. From resistance arise thoughts that confine and create ties that bind. A surrendered life, free from strife, receives the abundance that Source provides.

When we cut ourselves off from nature we lose sight of sound values and become steeped in blind materialism.

Celebrate your successes and accomplish-
ments, but do not take them seriously.
Neither success nor failure can be ours when
there is only One Life expressing.

Self-importance stemming from past accom-
plishments and pride of possessions blocks the
manifestation of greater things yet to come.

Do not lend empowerment through attention to financial doomsday predictions. Prepare for the worst and expect the best.

Where families have been supported by large debt structures, a necessary economic readjustment is to be expected. Substance must replace such hollowness. Forced change may not become necessary if, instead, we alter our lifestyles with dignity and grace.

If you desire flow to come to your life,
do not hoard. Donate that which you
do not use and throw away clutter.

There are those who seek to diminish your
resources and achievements and those who
try to profit from them. Neither believes they
can achieve through their own effort. Do not
allow them to become your ball and chain.

Enabling others to view you as their line
of credit is to promote disempowerment
and a misplaced sense of entitlement.

Do not support the worldview of those
who seek the most they can get, that you
may not be encumbered by parasitic ties.

Those who take in greed deplete not
only themselves, but others as well.

Taking resources for granted depletes them.
All things dwindle in the face of ingratitude.

When we approach anything with
the question of 'What is the most
I can get?', scarcity arises.

Adversity can teach us more than many years
of prosperity, but only if we enthusiasti-
cally pick up the gauntlet it throws down.

Our society lures us into debt as a way of life.
Resist this insanity as much as possible.
Your greatest asset is freedom.

Not only is debt a form of enslavement,
but it creates the unwholesome situation
where we do not own the food we eat or
the clothes we wear — the bank does.

All addictions are the result of self-abandonment. The addiction to spending is no different. Balanced spending comes from balanced living.

Life's fertility wanes when egocentricity is present. Spontaneous giving of the self creates an environment in which to flourish.

When our existence is consumed with duty,
the heart feels deprived and life
becomes impoverished. No amount of
money can compensate for that.

Do not hang back from knocking on
doors before you because you do not
know whether you would want to enter.
Wonderful surprises may lie beyond.

Failure is not lack of success,
it is being afraid to try.

Self-pity creates a downward spiral in our cir-
cumstances, since what we focus on increases.

Do not let your work dictate the pace of your life. Dedicate time slots in which you respond to its demands. In this way it does not become the master and you the slave.

Guilt over incurred debt blocks future flow. Any beneficial change requires acceptance of the present.

As conduits for the flow of Infinite resources, we should view ourselves as custodians rather than owners.

When previous financial systems fail us, looking for solutions within those systems seldom works. Think outside the box.

The soul justifies its excesses and indulgences
through self-pity. Uproot self-pity ruthlessly —
it obscures truth.

Self-pity looks outside itself to be rescued.
Self-responsibility finds a solution within.

Do not use money to substitute giving
of yourself, for it causes an imbalance
that creates lack for you and others.

Abundance in Relationship

Life may seem to be the One expressing as the many, but it is also the many expressing as the One. Each is all that is, and relationships therefore do not exist; they are roles we play to illustrate the infinite variety of expression within the One.

Relationships are like a river — their dynamics shift. Appraising them regularly is essential for the wellbeing of all.

In weathering the storms of relationship, the ability to love deepens for it is there we find and heal our shortcomings.

Learning to love without pain and live without agenda is humanity's greatest challenge.

Any relationship is an illusion within the One Life — even the inner relationship of the observer and the observed.

Other than Divine Compassion, all types of love are the sub-creations of man. Human love binds, Divine Compassion sets all potential free.

Blindness is born from loyalty. See others in your environment anew each day, that you not keep them captive by indulging their follies.

To love one more than another is like
loving an arm more than a leg. Both
are integral parts of the body.

You are not separate from another. Both are an
inter-related and merged field. Appearing separate is simply due to a peculiarity of vision.

Since all are obeying the song of the One
Life, all are expressing impeccably.

The only way relationship can truly be
sublimated is by knowing we reside
as one within the fullness of life.

Nothing can give or receive. There is no
passivity or pro-activity, no masculine
or feminine. Life in its wholeness
is experienced equally by all.

To suffer because of the hardship of others is
to imply that imperfection exists — that the
One Life cannot support Itself in a benign way.

Power is the result of not having relationship.
Relationship keeps static form in place.

Feelings are not pure as long as there
is identity. The heart cannot open
fully within identity's confines.

Comparisons and self-reflection create polarity. In turn, polarity creates the shadow of adversity.

Because of codependence, old doors stay open when they should be closed. New doors will not open until the old ones are shut.

One of the problems of relationship
is that we romanticize un-wholeness
and dysfunctionality.

To have relationship not founded in
Oneness is to abandon the self because it implies separation. Separation
denies the Source of our being.

When the inner child is not properly parented,
we seek uniformity through relationships even
when other areas of our life are in mastery.

True listening takes place in the absence of
thought. Only then can you enter into the experience of another's world. To truly listen to
someone is to assimilate a new perspective.

To avoid being caught in the social games
of others, the nurturing of them must
be done from the expanded self.

Lasting friendships must inspire mutual
growth if they are to be life-enhancing. The
only other way they could last is through
conformity — the death knell of greatness.

The most powerful manipulators are
those who choose to appear helpless and
inept. Those who fall into their traps
are the ones with a need to save.

Allowing those who are unsuccessful
in managing their own lives to manage
part of yours is as foolish as the patient
trying to treat the physician.

We can see in others either chaos or
Oneness. Whatever we choose to see, we
do not need to engage but to envelop.

Those who 'love' you while they are in ego-
consciousness cannot actually feel love for
you, because from such contracted vision
they cannot see you. Truly seeing you must
acknowledge your limitless divinity. In the
absence of this, only attachment can occur.

Abundant Peace
and Contentment

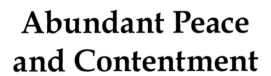

Lie back in the peaceful
arms of the One Life. Even
if the worst you fear comes
about, the loving arms of
the Infinite will lift you up
and over such hardships.

All reveals itself through the silent
surrender of our being.

Humility means we stand in silence
before the wonder of our being and
allow it to reveal everything to us.

In the quietness of the mind, life yields
all secrets to a receptive heart.

Confusion drains energy. When faced
with conflict or dilemma, choose to stay in
stillness until the answer reveals itself.

When the human soul feels alienated from
Source it seeks a situation that offers a sense
of 'belonging', as in a tribe. The tribe, however,
stunts growth because it requires conformity.
Solitude is the price of greatness.

In the absence of the dialogue of the mind,
all things are possible. Thoughts arise
from opposition to life. Let your mantra
therefore be: **I cease to oppose life**.

Power and innocence are two sides of
one coin. Innocence can only be found
by living in the moment. It is in the moment where power is found also.

Humans' greatest fear is their own inner
silence — the place where all unresolved
trauma reveals itself. Facing oneself in
silence is a threshold that must be crossed
for the peace of mastery to be birthed.

Meditation is the finger pointing at the moon. Reach for the moon and do not over-focus on the finger. Living with complete attention and surrender to the moment accomplishes this.

The heart does not open until the mind has been silenced. Only then will the infinite preciousness of life reveal itself.

Noise pulls us from this moment into the next, where linear time resides. Treasure moments of silence, they allow the tension of linear time to leave your body.

Create a sacred space by expressing passionately. The denser you find your environment, the greater the need to push the density back with your passion.

Humility is not to believe you are less than
another. That merely pays homage to the
other's arrogance. Humility is acknowledging that every life has equal value.

In the silent depths of our being, concepts
like power, movement and growth fall
away — yielding to rapturous peace.

The idle fill the air with chatter.
The master embraces in Silence the
contradiction of his being.

Suffering is only inherent in life when we
engage in its movement. In the stillness of full
surrender, we enter the peace of timelessness.

The mind creates mirrors then fights against them. When we wait in stillness, all life reveals itself to us.

Abundant resources become ours when we leave the movement of life, which is time. Through surrender, we become the still point and all comes to us.

Peace in the world comes from peace
within. Peace within comes from the
inner marriage of our masculine and
feminine into perfect oneness.

The key to stepping off the moving
wheel of linear time into the stillness of
the One Life, is to release the concept of
relationship through the understanding that there is only One Being.

As we awaken to our true heritage to
find we are all that is, we come directly
in touch with the magic of all life.

Living as the One Life is the greatest con-
tribution we can make to the whole.

The shallow accessing of life is no bet-
ter than engaging it deeply. All parts
of the ocean are equally valid.

There are no questions, only
unfolding revelations.

We think we discover the new, but what
we have discovered is the eternal newness
with which life expresses every moment.

Recognizing form to be a specific
emphasis of beingness allows us to
masterfully de-emphasize discordance
and emphasize harmony.

As life changes from a lower order to a higher one, power is released. Change is therefore the bringer of great gifts and should be welcomed.

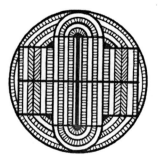

All you see that is praiseworthy can become an active part of you. If it were not already slumbering within, you would not be able to recognize it without.

Yeats said: *"Where beauty has no ebb, decay no flood, but joy is wisdom, time an endless song ..."*
But it is only in timelessness where the qualities he mentioned are found. Only there where the song of the Infinite expressing is not drowned out by the discordance of time.

Manifesting an Abundant Environment

Life empties itself every moment, only to be filled again. When we fluidly match this ever-new regeneration we can, through grateful enjoyment, call forth what makes our hearts sing.

In each light seeker's life is the knowledge
that they are all that is. To act in a way
that is life-enhancing to self benefits all.

There are only two choices in the
cosmos: what is more life-enhancing
and what is most life-enhancing.

Thought pulls us out of the moment into the past or future. It disturbs innocence, since innocence is only found in the moment.

A life well lived is like climbing a mountain; every new moment is the highest point of your life.

Some, unaware that they create their
own life experiences, say 'if only'. Others,
having refined themselves through
experiential wisdom, say, 'next time'.

Excellence cannot be an occasional
visitor. It has to be a constant companion.
It will then invite additional guests:
opportunity, success and increase.

Only the blind believe they have multiple choices in life. The wise know there is only one viable choice in every situation: that which is most life-enhancing.

A planned future is a closed future. Allow yourself to dream and plan, but leave enough room for life to surprise you.

The essence of abundant living is found in
generosity of expression, not in depleting our
environment by taking more than we need.

See life as a spontaneous dance of joy, not
a fixed maze through which you have
to find your way with perseverance.

Linear time and linear becoming have in reality never existed. We are free to powerfully effect the fluid unfolding of the moment through the purity of our intent without the bondage of time's delay between cause and effect.

To live an impeccable life promotes that which is life-enhancing for all.

What we focus on, we solidify. What
we experience without expectations
unfolds into endless possibilities.

Causes within the Dream do not create an
effect. The One Life does. When we cease trying to affect life, miracles flow through us.

We believe we can change independently
from our environment. But we are all
things. When we change, all changes.

Life around us lies in intermingled
fields of possibilities that come alive
only when the song of our lives
stimulates them into existence.

We often feel responsible for maintaining
harmony in our environment. From the
large picture there is only harmony,
thus nothing to maintain.

We hesitate to act before we can ensure
a beneficial outcome. All outcomes
are beneficial, for we dwell in the
benevolence of the Infinite.

No history exists. No future awaits. Just the moment that stretches into eternity.

Change as unfoldment can come in a moment. In knowing this, we can bring it about. Through the miracles of our lives we set others free as well.

Prayer has been used through eons to
fulfill our agendas. It is a redundant
concept when we are eternally guided
by the Infinite's song of perfection.

If we can live one moment gloriously, and
then the next and the next — greatness is
born. But it comes one choice at a time.

When we do everything from a sense
of great adventure, we are aligned with
the very purpose of created life.

Let us live life as a spontaneous expression, not as a set of guidelines
we need to know. Then at last our
futile search for truth will cease.

In ceasing to strive, the moment embraces
you. In seeing the perfection behind appearances, you enter through the gates of
timelessness where all becomes possible.

Let life be a living affirmation: Give liberally
of your praise, love and gratitude. Embrace
readily the new unfolding of life's adventure.

The Abundant Self

The dancing feet have no
volition of their own, but
are directed by the dancer.
Living from the greater self
restores abundant grace to
the life of the little self.

Become sensitive to your promptings from
within. Disregarding them and then blaming
external sources for your depletion, is not
masterful. Play when it is time, work when it
is required, for you write the script
of your own life.

Supported by all life, overwhelming
odds cannot exist. A master accesses
all perspectives at once.

The only discovery is self-discovery,
which we express through our
experiences as increased enjoyment.

Power is an irrevocably fused component of
the incorruptible holy matter from which we
are made. It is our inseparable birthright.

Roles can be assumed to aid in manifesting intent. They only obscure truth when we believe them to be all that we are.

The light-seeker is always ready to embrace the truth of the moment and to change directions in order to follow the adventure of self-discovery.

That which we seek to understand about ourselves is not that which is waiting to be learnt,
but that which is waiting to be expressed.

Choose as companions those who
make you feel augmented and who
inspire you to excel. As you grow,
shed with grace those who do not.

Masters do not rely on belief, but
rather on effortless knowing. The greatest stumbling blocks to learning are
belief systems and worldviews.

Masters have nothing to prove
and everything to discover.

You are the center of your cosmos. With all
the power of your vast existence, let every
touch and every word convey compassion and blessings. In this way you place
the crown of sovereignty on your head.

Regrets come only when growth has oc-
curred. Many would forfeit their past foolish
actions, but then the growth those actions
brought would have to be given up as well.
Embrace your seeming folly as your greatest gift — it was a teacher in disguise.

To forgive others assumes guilt. True forgiveness knows there is nothing to forgive.
No one can do anything to us without
our having called it in or agreed to it.

Trust comes from knowing we are connected
to Source. Courage comes from extending
beyond the boundaries of our comfort zone to
the place where all new knowledge is gained.

Most waste energy wishing their lives
would change. Masters change their environment by changing themselves.

A master cannot afford to indulge even
the smallest blind spot in his or her
vision. A grain of sand is not small
in the mechanism of a watch.

Character is formed one choice at a time. However, two ingredients are always present; firmness with oneself and gentleness with others.

If you pacify the petty tyrants of your life for the sake of keeping peace, you will instead be promoting tyranny. In failing to learn the lessons they come to impart, you keep them on their treadmill of being unpleasant perception givers.

What we attempt to control will produce
volatility instead. The only control
we may ever have is self-control.

There are those who build and those
who tear down. What makes the difference is not being afraid to fail.

A life of mastery is comprised of belief and faith. Believe in the infallibility of your actions as long as you live your highest truth. Faith knows that good intentions will ultimately benefit all.

We empower what we focus on. Define yourself through every action as the master you are and you shall surely embody it.

Total self-responsibility and absolute
freedom are two sides of one coin. One
cannot exist without the other.

The most immediate way to gain power
is to see what you have never seen before.
Seeing further than your surface mind can
grasp will set you free from its tyranny.

Feeling unlovable, many settle for feeling
needed. Lovingly parent your inner child,
for it is the birthplace of self-worth.

Because the cosmos is benign, there is
only one place where courage applies —
living from ruthless self-honesty.

Death has no place in the fabric of
existence — the incorruptible holy matter
of the Infinite's Being. The master savors
the one fluid moment that never ends.

All self-perception is a lens
into the Infinite's Being.

The consciousness of an individual is determined by how much of life's resources his attitudes permit him to access. All life consists of an infinite supply of resources.

Life is a grindstone. Whether it grinds you down or polishes you to a luster depends on what you are made of.

Laughing at yourself keeps you
from succumbing to the pompous
preening of self-importance.

In the adventure of life we are required to
perform many roles. In believing them to be
real, they become identities. Identity traps
awareness and hinders spiritual evolution.

If you would find your strong suits, seek them in your weaknesses. It is in overcoming them that your greatest strengths will be forged.

To masterfully create truth rather than seek it, one must live an extraordinary life beyond mortal boundaries.

The measure of a person is not how far down he has been, but how much he has overcome. Do not look back or you may define yourself by what you have been, rather than by what you are.

When needs are present, the heart is as much a tyrant as the mind and is an unreliable source of information. Onmi-sensory experience is a more reliable tool.

The greatest freedom to strive for is
the freedom from thinking that anything can be bound by the unreal.

We design the games of life by hiding parts
of perception; if you don't like the game,
reclaim the perception and play another.

Wisdom is the addiction of the master who,
having stepped beyond the existing paradigm,
uses it as a frame of reference. Afraid of his
own vastness, he reaches for yesterday's truth.

Fallacies and belief systems must be elimi-
nated; we assist others and ourselves by living
our highest truth in each moment.

Predictability is an obstacle to greatness
that binds us to past standards.

Planning creates a container or mold
for life to fill. Plans can become traps
when we rigidly hold onto them.

Leadership consists of self-responsibility.
All life can be changed through proxy
by one who knows this to be so. The
goal of life is that all become leaders.

Self-responsibility brings freedom, for
with it comes more self-determination.

To feel the support of the oneness of life, let our mantra be: "**The Earth is my cradle and the sky is my blanket. Wherever I go, I am home.**"

Knowing life to be a dream, we can become lucid dreamers — masters of the dream environment. Reality becomes fluid rather than static and a life of miracles ensues.

The initiate knows he can change his
environment by changing himself. The
master knows no difference, but en-
joys his environment as himself.

Self-confidence comes from the
ego-identification of the smaller self.
Self-trust comes from knowing our
infallibility as the One Life.

All programmed behavior must dissolve by allowing the fluid expression of the Infinite through us. This includes the conditioned expectations of how to express maleness or femaleness.

No one is truly free who wears the mask of identity. He becomes a puppet in the hands of others, who feed his ego-identification.

The all-knowledge and skill of the One Life is
ours to draw upon. That learning is needed
to accomplish excellence is an illusion.

The shadows in our lives are cast by un-
yielded potential — the result of living
a life of opposites. To live in oneness
is to live a shadowless existence.

The fear of making mistakes, coupled with
the realization that life is unknowable,
causes man to cling to fragments of
yesterday's truth. It is in self-trust as the
One Being that we release our doubts.

Because life moves through us, we have no
freedom of choice and hence no responsibility.
The concept of freedom is like the hand
saying to the body, "I want to be free".

The tribe is one of the timing mechanisms
of life. It tries to bind with conformity,
keeping individuals in mediocrity.
Those who wish to live in excellence
must break free from the tribe.

Structured programs of living, such as
social conditioning, act like viruses to life
and cause a dissonant reality. Observe
the origins of your actions to make sure
they do not arise from programming.

As long as any programming
exists in our lives, our feelings are
unreliable sources for conveying the
Infinite's unfoldment through us.

When we live a programmed life, like a
moth in a spider web, we cannot tell when
another strand of subliminal programming
captures us. Freedom from conditioning will
reveal the intrusion of another's thoughts.

The illumination that life is an experience,
not a set of guidelines to live by, dissolves
the prison erected by the need to know.

The absolute conviction that the One
Life is our unwavering support is our
passage to self-sovereignty. We live in
the timelessness of the One Life, freed
from the bondage of mind and space.

There can be no abandonment. The real
eternal part of us is at all times participating
in full knowingness throughout our lives.

Effortless knowing does not need to pacify
reason by proving itself. When the addictions
of expanded awareness and ego-identification
are removed, the graceful unfolding of
life without the need to know remains.

Fear of relinquishing the body is fear
of freedom, like a captive afraid of
the unknown outside his cell.

There is no need for overcoming past
illusions from our lives. Illusions are
merely a timing mechanism to guide us
through the dance. When it is time for
them to dissolve, it will be obvious.

There is a fear that the One Life's vastness is boring. But it needs to be experienced with more than our illusory perception for the indescribable glory to reveal itself.

The misperception that any part of life can be harmful comes from illusory belief systems. But they too are unreal — the ocean is always whole by nature.

The one whose identity is based on what he
does is like a traveler in an unknown land,
navigating the way forward by a map of
where he has been.

Our bodies cannot be incarcerated
when our spirits are free. We can
only be imprisoned by beliefs.

Responsibility can be like an identity carried like a heavy burden or a badge. We can become identified as someone who can be counted on. All identity traps awareness.

Conformity does not make the soul feel at home, but rather causes it to withdraw in pain. This strengthens materialism.

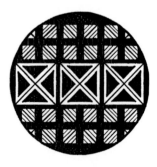

Addiction arises from self-abandonment. Mind abandons its inner knowingness by trying to understand through answers from without.

The difference between a conscious person and one who is not, is that in one the resources of life are latent, while in the other they are expressed.

How much consciousness we possess is
determined by how much we surrender
to life, not by how much we engage in
the mind-made trappings of holiness.

Life is a perfectly directed play and
every being plays his part. Even if
there is seeming apathy on the part of a
character, it is written into the script.

The timing of the dance of life is orchestrated
by what seem to be delays. But flawless is the
timing of the steps of the dance. Knowing this,
how can we be anything other than patient?

Abundance in Expression

We dwell within the Infinite's Being where all potential is immediately available to the extent we are willing to receive it. The necessity to grow is a fallacy. Surrendered allowing is the criterion of fulfilled mastery.

Trauma as a way of growth is contradic-
tory. If the aim of growth is oneness,
trauma cannot deliver it for hardship is the result of separation.

Linear growth is of the mind. Exponential
growth comes in an instant through
the flowering of the heart. Growth is
not gained through overcomings,
but by embracing wholeness.

Opposition delivers perception. But if we do
not take time to integrate the perception, it
damages the heart. In the stillness of mind
the heart finds its peace.

There is nothing that constitutes testing.
We do not have to prove our right to exist
when we are an expression of Infinite Life.

Rage, fear, pain, protectiveness and guilt
are but the backward images of pure
emotions reflected in the mirrored walls
of our chrysalis of belief systems.

Blame and forgiveness are two sides
of one coin. Both are born of blindness
to the innocence of all experience.

The unenlightened oppose others, expecting to
be opposed themselves. The master supports
others in that he knows them to be himself.

Aloneness yields strength. Aware
interaction with others yields warmth.
Both are needed for wholeness.

Bodily appetites are like an unruly child and must be schooled to know their place, not as needs, but merely as optional desires.

It is not death that kills, but opposition to life. Many say they do not want to die, but few have ever really lived.

To fear is to abandon the sovereign perfection of the self, creating emptiness within.
Nature cannot abide a vacuum, thus what
we fear is attracted to fill the empty space.

Accepting the unacceptable is not saintly;
it is dysfunctional. It is your sacred duty to
treat with reverence the divine heritage you
have received from the Infinite's hand.

Power and perception are inseparably connected. To seek perception, while with false
humility shunning power, is a contradiction.

The correlation between energy and consciousness demands that you treat your
energy as a priceless possession. To squander
energy is to disrespect consciousness.

To fulfill your heart's desires before those
of someone else allows you to give to
others from a position of wholeness.

When we abandon ourselves, the tendency
to define ourselves by what we are not
becomes strong. Anything that defines
itself by its opposite is an illusion.

In a life of no opposites, when the directions come home to the heart and linearity is no more, we become the door of everything.

The body is a dispensable field that can be replaced by another. It is but a servant. The real part of us is the master.

Healing duality does not mean ending
the song by playing all the notes at once,
but by having each note that is played
reflect the whole within it. Let each
action be a tribute to the One Life.

The body is re-shaped by our living in
the One Life. The aged may youthen, the
care-worn become filled with lightness
of being. It is an instrument of delight.

A physical parting cannot occur
since the true essence of all beings
is like an intermingled field.

When we dwell in separation, the body's false
claim to be the self is fed by its demands for
attention. When we remember we are one
the body that is unreal dissolves, revealing the incorruptible form of eternal life.

Bodily depletion is an illusion that will vanish
when we see ourselves as living from the
place of no-time where life is always renewed.

The perfection of life cannot be tarnished.
There is nothing but self-regulating wholeness.
The eons of seeming illusion are nothing but
the oyster that opens to reveal the pearl.

Our wholeness cannot be tainted when
we live life from the perfection of
Beingness. The illusory life of form is
then a malleable tool to the One Life.

As unique expressions of the Infinite,
eternal yet ever new, our bodies are
sacred. Let us honor these instruments
of grace as living temples of divinity.

Separation causes self-reflection and comparison. These in turn cause self-pity or self-importance. In recognizing oneness, the beauty and admirable qualities of all become ours.

Suffering is not the tool of discipline, nor the test of worthiness. It is the result of opposition to life.

By imagining ourselves as being the mind, the emotions and the body, we believe that loss can be a reality: like a child crying for its mother who is in another room. By knowing ourselves as the eternal vastness containing all, separation cannot occur.

The mind, unlike the heart, can only draw its conclusions from face values. Discernment is born of the heart. Judgment is of the mind.

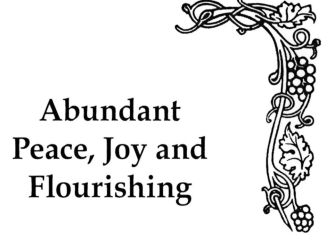

Abundant Peace, Joy and Flourishing

Allowing our unfettered, wildish parts to innocently express dissolves the inclination to be imprisoned by other's approval and trapped by social expectations.

All mysteries are already known to the
Infinite. Our quest for freedom from the
dream has been fulfilled. There is nothing
to solve and no duty, just the joy of living.

When oneness creates a life of not opposites,
equilibrium is the nature of reality. From
the soil of equilibrium, flowering occurs.

Mastery demands that we live outside
the confines of the masses' world views;
that we stand upon the shoulders of
previously revered masters and fly.

The disciplined master does not treat the
past as real by looking back. Time does not
exist. All knowledge reveals itself when
we stay in the moment within silence of
the mind. This is effortless knowing.

Life is not a process of seeking to become.
It is instead a flowering of where we are.
Light-seekers diligently weed the garden
of the soul, but often forget to sow the
seeds of contentment and delight.

In seeking to eliminate our flaws, life
becomes depleted unless the gaps they
leave are filled. It is in the laughter of the
heart that seeds of potential grow.

Many dream of a point of arrival for their
journey, neglecting to see that the only point of
arrival is the present. Imagination is inspired
by acknowledging the gifts of the moment.

Contentment arises from the knowledge
that wherever we are in the moment
has taken eons to achieve and is
therefore our greatest gift.

If tomorrow is forged by this moment, but this
moment is spent living in the future, where
will tomorrow come from?

When deep elation fills your soul,
you have just lived your highest truth.

To seek truth within already existing belief systems is to swim around and around the walls of our self-made fish bowl. Only in the silence of the mind can original thinking take place.

When life is a living work of art, the whisperings of source express through all we do. Art bypasses the conscious and sub-conscious minds as a non-cognitive communication from the Infinite.

Do not fear adversity. What is a symphony without its low notes? When the storm winds blow through the seasons of your life, the loving embrace of the Infinite will shelter you.

The highest form of compassion is to surround yourself with those who inspire joy and to interact sparingly with those who do not. Because opposite frequency attracts, your joy will automatically be attracted to the most joyless place on earth.

Fulfillment begins by rejoicing in what
you have. Change begins in accepting
where you are. Increase begins in
being grateful for your supply.

If you have become a stranger to passion,
find its tracks within your joy. The deeper
you go into joy, the more your passion
will reveal itself, for they are partners
in the wondrous discovery of life.

Obstacles are but the illusory guidelines
that direct the steps of the dance of
life. We can also use the more pleasant
method of following our joy.

In our fellow man and all around us, the
praiseworthy lies like the gems of dewdrops
on a spider-web, waiting to be discovered.

Living vibrantly gives others permission to do so also. It furthermore creates a resonance within them that awakens their own vibrancy.

Beauty can only be seen when the mind is still and the heart is open. What is beauty but the momentary glimpse of Eternity?

No external approval is needed, for we
have been created for the sake of
delight. There is nothing to accomplish
other than deep enjoyment of life.

Through us the One Life expresses flawlessly
and in spite of ourselves. The gentle violin
and the thunderous drums have equally
important parts in the symphony.

The seeming happiness of those living
on the treadmill of life is an illusion.
Happiness is not fulfillment of our desires,
but fulfillment without having desires.

The tendency to label parts of life in order
to pacify reason and provide the illusion of
predictability enslaves us to form. To circum-
vent this, we experience life with complete
attention to the moment, freely acknowledging that because everything is renewed in
every moment, we can know nothing.

Genius has no intellect. It is present
in the master who has achieved
emptiness of mind through complete
surrender, as effortless knowing.

As life moves through us, its dance can be
performed with enjoyment or resistance.
Enjoyment comes from the contentment that
results from surrender.

Humor is the experience of enter-
ing into the rapture of the movement
of the One Life. Laughter is the release
of such a momentous experience.

We are not needed by the Infinite to
help shape life, but rather given the
opportunity to share in the joy.

Complexity and simplicity in fact do not exist.
There is only the unfolding of Beingness that
defies description as it unfolds in its splendor.

Life is a dance of tranquility and revelry,
filled with the merry madness of delight.

Understanding life is not possible if we
realize that there is no preconceived plan
of expression, but rather a spontaneous
display of the Infinite's self-enjoyment.

Bringing gifts of joy to another is nothing
more than becoming an open channel
for life flowing through itself.

It is in quietness and surrendered contentment that we access the true wealth of our being — the perfection lying like diamonds in the dust of belief systems.

In contented surrender and peace, our joyful expectations are surpassed.

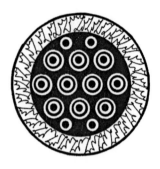

All perception is really self-perception
because you can only recognize
that which is within you.

To allow others to affect the quality of
your day is to navigate your life like a
rudderless ship, subject to being tossed
about by the shifting breezes.

In living from your highest identity as a consciousness superimposed over all that is, the cosmos becomes your resource library. Breathe in the timelessness of the stars, the newness of the dawn, the fluid grace of the river.

Closing

Q.   *What is the value of wisdom when the more I seek it, the less I know?*

A.   The worth of wisdom is that the seeker discovers that around in a circle he goes. The greatest gift that wisdom can give is its own illusions to show.

Q.   *What lies beyond wisdom that I can seek and ultimately hope to find?*

A.   The ending of wisdom is the beginning of the contradiction of life.

Q.   *I hear it shine through wisdom's words, yet no description of the One Life have I heard.*

A.   That which is real cannot be described, for it lies beyond the confines of understanding.

Q.   *Then how shall I know the Infinite's voice?*

A.   The song of the Infinite is all there is. To interpret it, you have no choice. Thus seek not to understand, for no creation can, the glorious paradox of life. Cease to strive, but dance with delight to the song of eternal life.

For more information, see
http://alminediary.com,
http://www.facebook.com/SeersWisdom
and http://twitter.com/alminewisdom

Also by Almine
The Seer's Journey

This moving, lyrical work — reminiscent of Khahil Gibran's *The Prophet* — provides an intimate and revealing glimpse into this renowned mystic's search for the truth behind the creation of man. Almine's worldwide audience will cherish *The Seer's Journey*, sharing her journey as she explores the purpose of life through the translations of the Scrolls of Infinity. This may be the most significant information yet produced by this author.

Published 2009, 124 pages, hardcover, 6x9, ISBN 978-1-934070-46-8

Almine is the author of 11 other books. All are available on http://www.spiritualjourneys.com

LaVergne, TN USA
20 May 2010
183385LV00002B/2/P